My Journal

ORDER MY STEPS

This Book Belongs To:

_____

Year: _____

Unless otherwise indicated,
scripture quotations are from the
New International Version of the Bible.

© 2014 Encouraging Pen Publications
www.encouragingpen.com
ISBN-13: 978-1503107939
ISBN-10: 1503107930

Thy word is a lamp unto my feet, and a light unto my path.

Psalm 119:105

Why I Chose This Word

What I Believe God Wants to Do In and Through Me

Order my steps in thy word: and let not any iniquity have dominion over me.

Psalm 119:133 (KJV)

A man's steps are established by the Lord, and He takes pleasure in his way. Though he falls, he will not be overwhelmed because the Lord holds his hand.

> Psalm 37:27 (HCSB)

He restores my soul; He leads me in the paths of righteousness For His name's sake.

Psalm 23:3

You will show me the path of life; In Your presence is fullness of joy; At Your right hand are pleasures forevermore.

                              Psalm 16:11

My steps have held to your paths; my feet have not stumbled.

> Psalm 17:5

Thy word is a lamp unto my feet, and a light unto my path.

Psalm119:105 (KJV)

In all thy ways acknowledge him, and he shall direct thy paths.

Proverbs 3:6 (KJV)

Lord, lead me as you promised me you would; otherwise my enemies will conquer me. Tell me clearly what to do, which way to turn.

Psalm 5:8 (TLB)

And I will lead the blind in a way that they do not know, in paths that they have not known I will guide them. I will turn the darkness before them into light, the rough places into level ground. These are the things I do, and I do not forsake them.

                              Isaiah 42:16 (ESV)

Cause me to hear Your lovingkindness in the morning, For in You do I trust; Cause me to know the way in which I should walk, For I lift up my soul to You.

                              Psalm 143:8 (NKJV)

The Lord will watch over your coming and going both now and forevermore.

Psalm 121:8

For we walk by faith, not by sight.

2 Corinthians 5:7 (NKJV)

"For I know the plans I have for you," declares the Lord, "plans to prosper you and not to harm you, plans to give you hope and a future."

Jeremiah 29:11

"I am the Lord your God, who teaches you what is best for you, who directs you in the way you should go."

Isaiah 48:17

Don't be afraid, for the Lord will go before you and will be with you; he will not fail nor forsake you.

Deuteronomy 31:8 (TLB)

You have made known to me the paths of life;
you will fill me with joy in your presence.

Acts 2:28

Order my steps in thy word: and let not any iniquity have dominion over me.

Psalm 119:133 (KJV)

A man's steps are established by the Lord, and He takes pleasure in his way. Though he falls, he will not be overwhelmed because the Lord holds his hand.

Psalm 37:27 (HCSB)

He restores my soul; He leads me in the paths of righteousness For His name's sake.

Psalm 23:3

You will show me the path of life; In Your presence is fullness of joy; At Your right hand are pleasures forevermore.

                                            Psalm 16:11

My steps have held to your paths; my feet have not stumbled.

Psalm 17:5

Thy word is a lamp unto my feet, and a light unto my path.

Psalm119:105 (KJV)

In all thy ways acknowledge him, and he shall direct thy paths.

Proverbs 3:6 (KJV)

Lord, lead me as you promised me you would; otherwise my enemies will conquer me. Tell me clearly what to do, which way to turn.

                                        Psalm 5:8 (TLB)

And I will lead the blind in a way that they do not know, in paths that they have not known I will guide them. I will turn the darkness before them into light, the rough places into level ground. These are the things I do, and I do not forsake them.

Isaiah 42:16 (ESV)

Cause me to hear Your lovingkindness in the morning, For in You do I trust; Cause me to know the way in which I should walk, For I lift up my soul to You.

Psalm 143:8 (NKJV)

The Lord will watch over your coming and going both now and forevermore.

> Psalm 121:8

For we walk by faith, not by sight.

2 Corinthians 5:7 (NKJV)

"For I know the plans I have for you," declares the Lord, "plans to prosper you and not to harm you, plans to give you hope and a future."

Jeremiah 29:11

"I am the Lord your God, who teaches you what is best for you, who directs you in the way you should go."

Isaiah 48:17

Don't be afraid, for the Lord will go before you and will be with you; he will not fail nor forsake you.

Deuteronomy 31:8 (TLB)

You have made known to me the paths of life;
you will fill me with joy in your presence.

Acts 2:28

Order my steps in thy word: and let not any iniquity have dominion over me.

Psalm 119:133 (KJV)

A man's steps are established by the Lord, and He takes pleasure in his way. Though he falls, he will not be overwhelmed because the Lord holds his hand.

Psalm 37:27 (HCSB)

He restores my soul; He leads me in the paths of righteousness For His name's sake.

Psalm 23:3

You will show me the path of life; In Your presence is fullness of joy; At Your right hand are pleasures forevermore.

Psalm 16:11

My steps have held to your paths; my feet have not stumbled.

Psalm 17:5

Thy word is a lamp unto my feet, and a light unto my path.

Psalm 119:105 (KJV)

In all thy ways acknowledge him, and he shall direct thy paths.

Proverbs 3:6 (KJV)

Lord, lead me as you promised me you would; otherwise my enemies will conquer me. Tell me clearly what to do, which way to turn.

> Psalm 5:8 (TLB)

And I will lead the blind in a way that they do not know, in paths that they have not known I will guide them. I will turn the darkness before them into light, the rough places into level ground. These are the things I do, and I do not forsake them.

Isaiah 42:16 (ESV)

Cause me to hear Your lovingkindness in the morning, For in You do I trust; Cause me to know the way in which I should walk, For I lift up my soul to You.

Psalm 143:8 (NKJV)

The Lord will watch over your coming and going both now and forevermore.

Psalm 121:8

For we walk by faith, not by sight.

2 Corinthians 5:7 (NKJV)

"For I know the plans I have for you," declares the Lord, "plans to prosper you and not to harm you, plans to give you hope and a future."

Jeremiah 29:11

"'I am the Lord your God, who teaches you what is best for you, who directs you in the way you should go."

Isaiah 48:17

Don't be afraid, for the Lord will go before you and will be with you; he will not fail nor forsake you.

Deuteronomy 31:8 (TLB)

You have made known to me the paths of life;
you will fill me with joy in your presence.

Acts 2:28

Order my steps in thy word: and let not any iniquity have dominion over me.

Psalm 119:133 (KJV)

A man's steps are established by the Lord, and He takes pleasure in his way. Though he falls, he will not be overwhelmed because the Lord holds his hand.

Psalm 37:27 (HCSB)

He restores my soul; He leads me in the paths of righteousness For His name's sake.

Psalm 23:3

You will show me the path of life; In Your presence is fullness of joy; At Your right hand are pleasures forevermore.

      Psalm 16:11

My steps have held to your paths; my feet have not stumbled.

Psalm 17:5

Thy word is a lamp unto my feet, and a light unto my path.

Psalm 119:105 (KJV)

In all thy ways acknowledge him, and he shall direct thy paths.

Proverbs 3:6 (KJV)

Lord, lead me as you promised me you would; otherwise my enemies will conquer me. Tell me clearly what to do, which way to turn.

Psalm 5:8 (TLB)

And I will lead the blind in a way that they do not know, in paths that they have not known I will guide them. I will turn the darkness before them into light, the rough places into level ground. These are the things I do, and I do not forsake them.

Isaiah 42:16 (ESV)

Cause me to hear Your lovingkindness in the morning, For in You do I trust; Cause me to know the way in which I should walk, For I lift up my soul to You.

Psalm 143:8 (NKJV)

The Lord will watch over your coming and going both now and forevermore.

> Psalm 121:8

For we walk by faith, not by sight.

2 Corinthians 5:7 (NKJV)

"For I know the plans I have for you," declares the Lord, "plans to prosper you and not to harm you, plans to give you hope and a future."

Jeremiah 29:11

"I am the Lord your God, who teaches you what is best for you, who directs you in the way you should go."

Isaiah 48:17

Don't be afraid, for the Lord will go before you and will be with you; he will not fail nor forsake you.

Deuteronomy 31:8 (TLB)

You have made known to me the paths of life;
you will fill me with joy in your presence.

Acts 2:28

Order my steps in thy word: and let not any iniquity have dominion over me.

Psalm 119:133 (KJV)

A man's steps are established by the Lord, and He takes pleasure in his way. Though he falls, he will not be overwhelmed because the Lord holds his hand.

Psalm 37:27 (HCSB)

He restores my soul; He leads me in the paths of righteousness For His name's sake.

                              Psalm 23:3

You will show me the path of life; In Your presence is fullness of joy; At Your right hand are pleasures forevermore.

                    Psalm 16:11

My steps have held to your paths; my feet have not stumbled.

Psalm 17:5

Thy word is a lamp unto my feet, and a light unto my path.

Psalm 119:105 (KJV)

In all thy ways acknowledge him, and he shall direct thy paths.

Proverbs 3:6 (KJV)

Lord, lead me as you promised me you would; otherwise my enemies will conquer me. Tell me clearly what to do, which way to turn.

Psalm 5:8 (TLB)

And I will lead the blind in a way that they do not know, in paths that they have not known I will guide them. I will turn the darkness before them into light, the rough places into level ground. These are the things I do, and I do not forsake them.

Isaiah 42:16 (ESV)

Cause me to hear Your lovingkindness in the morning, For in You do I trust; Cause me to know the way in which I should walk, For I lift up my soul to You.

Psalm 143:8 (NKJV)

The Lord will watch over your coming and going both now and forevermore.

Psalm 121:8

For we walk by faith, not by sight.

2 Corinthians 5:7 (NKJV)

"For I know the plans I have for you," declares the Lord, "plans to prosper you and not to harm you, plans to give you hope and a future."

Jeremiah 29:11

"I am the Lord your God, who teaches you what is best for you, who directs you in the way you should go."

Isaiah 48:17

Don't be afraid, for the Lord will go before you and will be with you; he will not fail nor forsake you.

Deuteronomy 31:8 (TLB)

You have made known to me the paths of life;
you will fill me with joy in your presence.

Acts 2:28

Date

I'm Praying About

How This Prayer Was Answered

Date

I'm Praying About

How This Prayer Was Answered

Date

I'm Praying About

How This Prayer Was Answered

Date

I'm Praying About

How This Prayer Was Answered

How my One Word impacted my life over this past year

How my One Word impacted others

For more My One Word Journal titles, visit www.encouragingpen.com

Made in the USA
Monee, IL
20 January 2022